ELEVEN PLUS PRACTICE PAPERS

VERBAL REASONING

A | F | N
Publishing

AFN Publishing
2000

First published in Great Britain in 2000 by:

AFN Publishing
PO Box 1558
Gerrards Cross
Buckinghamshire
SL9 0XL

ISBN 0-9538487-0-1

Guidance Notes for Parents

The Practice Papers contained in this book are designed to introduce children to the types of questions found on 11 plus secondary school selection tests and to provide the opportunity to develop techniques for answering them.

It is important that your child's confidence is developed by working through the Practice Papers and the following suggested approach will help to achieve this.

The Progress Record Sheet at the end of the book can be used to monitor your child's progress.

Practice Paper 1

Read through the instructions on the Practice Paper with your child and explain what is required. It is recommended that you work through the first Practice Paper with your child without timing the exercise. Whilst working through the Practice Paper explain what the questions are asking you to do and what techniques should be used to answer them. You do not necessarily need to go through the whole Practice Paper at one time and you may want to divide the Practice Paper so that it can be covered in more manageable sessions.

Practice Paper 2

Let your child work through the second Practice Paper alone, again without timing. However, ensure that you are available to answer queries and to help if your child gets stuck on a particular type of question. After marking the Practice Paper go through any questions that your child has got wrong and explain how they should have been answered. Explain the technique again and ensure that your child understands what the question is asking for.

Remember to give recognition for correct answers.

Practice Paper 3

For Practice Paper 3 you should time your child. Encourage your child not to spend too much time on any one question but to keep up the momentum by leaving out questions that he or she is unsure of. Missed questions can be returned to at the end, if there is time.

After 50 minutes draw a line to show how far through the Practice Paper your child managed to get. This will allow you to identify how many questions your child was able to answer in the time available. However, allow your child to continue to the end of the Practice Paper before marking it.

After marking the Practice Paper, review the techniques used to answer the questions with your child to identify whether any improvements can be made.

Practice Papers 4 & 5

The aim of Practice Papers 4 and 5 should be to practise technique and to increase your child's accuracy and speed. You should therefore time these Practice Papers and encourage your child to monitor the time themselves so that they are aware of their own progress - this will be very important in the actual examinations.

After 50 minutes draw a line underneath the last question your child has answered so that you know how far he or she managed to get in the time allowed. After drawing the line, allow your child to complete the Practice Paper.

When you have marked a Practice Paper, work through any questions that your child may have got wrong and review the technique used. Again provide recognition for the correctly answered questions and for overall effort.

Practice Paper 1

(Verbal Reasoning)

Please complete these details before you begin:

Date: ....

Your Name: ....

Date of Birth: ....

School: ....

Please read the following before you start the Practice Paper:

1. Do not begin the Practice Paper until you are told to do so.

2. The Practice Paper contains 100 questions and you have 50 minutes to complete it.

3. Read the questions carefully so that you know what to do.

4. Try and answer as many questions as you can. You may not be able to answer all of them, so if you cannot answer a question go on to the next one. Do not spend too much time on one question.

5. Write your answers clearly. If you want to change an answer, put a single line through the wrong answer and write the correct answer clearly.

6. When you get to the end of the Practice Paper, go back and check your answers.

In the sentences below a four letter word is hidden at the end of one word and the start of the next word. Write the four letter word in the brackets. You must not change the order of the letters.

Example: The astronaut was wearing a spacesuit.   [**east**]

1. The armada was ready to sail.   [   ]   1.   ....

2. Do you have pens and pencils?   [   ]   2.   ....

3. They especially liked big chocolate bars.   [   ]   3.   ....

4. The shops close at five o'clock.   [   ]   4.   ....

5. All the sweets have been eaten.   [   ]   5.   ....

6. She recently bought a fluffy hamster.   [   ]   6.   ....

7. It's now beginning to rain again.   [   ]   7.   ....

In the questions below you must move one letter from the word on the left to the word on the right to make two new words. You are only allowed to move one letter and must not re-arrange any of the other letters. Write both new words in the brackets.

Example:

BROAD   OWL   [**Road**]   [**Bowl**]

8. FRIGHT   ICE   [   ]   [   ]   8.   ....

9. HEART   HEM   [   ]   [   ]   9.   ....

10. BEACH   TALE   [   ]   [   ]   10.   ....

11. MOUTH   PROD   [   ]   [   ]   11.   ....

12. BARROW   RAIN   [   ]   [   ]   12.   ....

13. THEIR   SEAM   [   ]   [   ]   13.   ....

14. BRIGHT   OLD   [   ]   [   ]   14.   ....

	✓	This page
Total		14

PLEASE CONTINUE ON THE NEXT PAGE

In the questions below underline **two** words, one from each group, that are **similar** in meaning.

Example: [<u>real</u>, pretend, unsure]   [<u>actual</u>, relax, ready]

15.	[scrape, raise, must]	[lower, graze, scope]	15.	....
16.	[start, cease, present]	[repeat, alert, stop]	16.	....
17.	[descend, higher, mountain]	[design, fall, climb]	17.	....
18.	[gleam, dull, dark]	[dream, glisten, cold]	18.	....
19.	[helpful, describe, seek]	[hide, alert, explain]	19.	....
20.	[broad, low, weigh]	[tall, wide, high]	20.	....
21.	[post, envelope, reply]	[write, answer, letter]	21.	....
22.	[referee, competitor, crowd]	[contestant, cricket, match]	22.	....

In the questions below underline **two** words, one from each group, that make a new word when combined. The word from the group on the left must come first.

Example: [<u>ant</u>, rice, when]   [find, hope, <u>elope</u>]

23.	[quiz, hold, fare]	[cycle, well, know]	23.	....
24.	[girl, clam, state]	[our, shine, find]	24.	....
25.	[assist, bright, deter]	[mined, step, lost]	25.	....
26.	[time, port, beg]	[sold, down, in]	26.	....
27.	[happy, cart, side]	[ridge, run, ride]	27.	....
28.	[cream, start, shop]	[stride, look, ping]	28.	....
29.	[tar, fire, dark]	[get, reach, wind]	29.	....
30.	[for, four, gold]	[date, help, tune]	30.	....

PLEASE CONTINUE ON THE NEXT PAGE

Total

✓	This page
	16

In the following questions, numbers have been replaced with letters. Work out the answer to the sum and write this in the brackets.

Example: If A = 6, B = 4, C = 2 and D = 1, find the answer to this sum, and **write it as a number**.

A + B + D = [**11**]

31. If A = 5, B = 4, C = 3 and D = 2, find the answer to this sum, and **write it as a number**.

A - C + D = [   ]

31. ....

32. If A = 6, B = 12, C = 24 and D = 48, find the answer to this sum, and **write it as a number**.

C ÷ B x D = [   ]

32. ....

33. If A = 2, B = 5, C = 10 and D = 20, find the answer to this sum, and **write it as a number**.

A x B x D = [   ]

33. ....

34. If A = 7, B = 8, C = 9 and D = 10, find the answer to this sum, and **write it as a number**.

A + B + C - D = [   ]

34. ....

35. If A = 11, B = 12, C = 13 and D = 14, find the answer to this sum, and **write it as a number**.

A + C - D = [   ]

35. ....

36. If A = 6, B = 4, C = 10 and D = 20, find the answer to this sum, and **write it as a number**.

A + B - C = [   ]

36. ....

37. If A = 20, B = 15, C = 10 and D = 5, find the answer to this sum, and **write it as a number**.

A - B - D = [   ]

37. ....

38. If A = 5, B = 10, C = 20 and D = 50, find the answer to this sum, and **write it as a number**.

B ÷ A x D = [   ]

38. ....

✓	This page
Total	8

PLEASE CONTINUE ON THE NEXT PAGE

There are four words and three codes written below. The codes are in a different order to the words and one code is missing. $E = 3$

MIND   DINE   MEAL   FAIL
  2763   8475   9345

Write the answer to the questions below in the brackets.

39.	What is the code number for FIND?	[ ]	39.	....
40.	Which word has the code number 8423?	[ ]	40.	....
41.	What is the code number for DALE?	[ ]	41.	....
42.	Which word has the code number 5348?	[ ]	42.	....
43.	What is the code number for LAME?	[ ]	43.	....
44.	Which word has the code number 5463?	[ ]	44.	....

45.   Andrew, Josephine and Nicholas need £3.00 each to see a film at the cinema.

Nicholas has £2.75.

Andrew and Josephine both have more money than Nicholas.

Which one of the following must be true? Write your answer in the brackets.

A. Andrew, Josephine and Nicholas all see the film.
B. Andrew has more money than Josephine.
C. Andrew and Josephine didn't see the film.
D. Nicholas couldn't see the film.
E. Andrew and Josephine both see the film.   [   ]   45. ....

46.   Anthony, Francesca, Nicola, Maria and Carlos all play hockey.
Anthony and Maria play football and golf.
Francesca plays golf and often plays lacrosse.
Francesca, Anthony, and Nicola play tennis and basketball.
Carlos and Maria play rugby.

Who plays the fewest sports?   [   ]   46. ....

PLEASE CONTINUE ON THE NEXT PAGE

✓	This page
Total	8

In the following questions the word which has been underlined has had three consecutive letters removed. These three letters make a correctly spelt word without being rearranged. Write the three-letter word in the brackets.

Example: The snake was extremely poious.   [**son**]

47. The girls got a <u>red</u> for finding the missing purse.   [   ]   47. ....

48. He <u>tped</u> over the kerb.   [   ]   48. ....

49. The <u>bge</u> was built in the nineteenth century.   [   ]   49. ....

50. The children <u>lised</u> to the story.   [   ]   50. ....

51. The ballerina was late for <u>rehsals</u>.   [   ]   51. ....

52. The house was owned by a <u>mionaire</u>.   [   ]   52. ....

53. The leopard was <u>hig</u> in the bushes.   [   ]   53. ....

Using the alphabet shown below, identify the next letters in the sequences and write them in the brackets.

A B C D E F G H I J K L M N O P Q R S T U V W X Y Z

Example: CD, FG, IJ, LM, [*OP*]

54. CH, EJ, GL, IN, KP,   [   ]   54. ....

55. XK, UM, RO, OQ, LS, IU,   [   ]   55. ....

56. HO, IP, GN, JQ, FM,   [   ]   56. ....

57. KK, LL, MN, NQ, OU, PZ,   [   ]   57. ....

58. CX, EV, GT, IR, KP,   [   ]   58. ....

59. KY, PT, UO, ZJ, EE,   [   ]   59. ....

60. PM, PQ, ST, SV, VW,   [   ]   60. ....

✓	This page
Total	14

PLEASE CONTINUE ON THE NEXT PAGE

In the questions below the **same** letter comes at the end of one word and the start of the other. The **same** letter must fit in both sets of brackets. Find the letter and write this in the brackets.

Example: rea [D] raw   plo [D] ame

61.	sta [ ] ent	ker [ ] ear	61. ....
62.	car [ ] old	moa [ ] ied	62. ....
63.	col [ ] ear	sla [ ] ime	63. ....
64.	lea [ ] law	gol [ ] ind	64. ....
65.	pai [ ] ame	foo [ ] ist	65. ....
66.	gna [ ] and	cro [ ] ant	66. ....
67.	goa [ ] ent	pes [ ] oad	67. ....
68.	dec [ ] not	bea [ ] ite	68. ....

In the following questions, calculate the number that will complete the sum and put your answer in the brackets.

Example: 8 + 3 = 2 + ?   [9]

69.	6 x 3 ÷ 2 = 4 x 6 - ?	[ ]	69. ....
70.	17 + 4 - 2 = 6 + 13 + ?	[ ]	70. ....
71.	18 x 6 = 3 x 20 + ?	[ ]	71. ....
72.	54 ÷ 18 + 27 = 80 ÷ 2 - ?	[ ]	72. ....
73.	30 x 4 - 81 = 7 x 6 - ?	[ ]	73. ....
74.	150 ÷ 5 - 4 = 3 x 7 + ?	[ ]	74. ....
75.	121 ÷ 11 + 11 = 4 x 3 + ?	[ ]	75. ....

PLEASE CONTINUE ON THE NEXT PAGE

	✓	This page
Total		15

In the following questions some of the words have been written in code. In each question the code has been "broken" for one word. You must use the same code to work out the second word and write the answer in the brackets.

The alphabet has been printed to help you.

A B C D E F G H I J K L M N O P Q R S T U V W X Y Z

Example: If GNLD means HOME, what does GDKO mean? [**HELP**]

76. If ODPS is the code for LAMP,
    what is the code for RICE? [   ]

77. If GVVRK means APPLE,
    what does LXAOZ mean? [   ]

78. If BMARMP is the code for DOCTOR,
    what is the code for NURSES? [   ]

79. If ALEPI is the code for WHALE,
    what is the code for MOUSE? [   ]

80. If YUIIKX means SOCCER,
    what does VRGEKX mean? [   ]

81. If GCWLJX is the code for FATHER,
    what is the code for MOTHER? [   ]

82. If GQDP means FOAL,
    what does NQOI mean? [   ]

83. If RWVDU is the code for TABLE,
    what is the code for SLIME? [   ]

84. If FORTQ means CROWN,
    what does EXGDH mean? [   ]

76. ....
77. ....
78. ....
79. ....
80. ....
81. ....
82. ....
83. ....
84. ....

PLEASE CONTINUE ON THE NEXT PAGE

✓	This page
Total	9

In the questions below write the number in the brackets that continues the sequence.

Example: 3, 6, 9, 12, [**15**]

85.	2, 7, 12, 17, 22,	[ ]	85. ....
86.	21, 19, 17, 15, 13,	[ ]	86. ....
87.	1, 2, 4, 8,	[ ]	87. ....
88.	11, 6, 13, 9, 15, 12,	[ ]	88. ....
89.	11, 19, 12, 17, 14, 14, 17,	[ ]	89. ....
90.	2, 4, 12, 48,	[ ]	90. ....
91.	1, 4, 10, 22,	[ ]	91. ....
92.	22, 17, 21, 18, 20,	[ ]	92. ....

In the following questions there are two groups of words. The word in brackets on the left-hand side has been formed in a certain way using letters from the other words on the left-hand side. Use the letters in the words on the right-hand side to form a word **in the same way**. Write your answer in the brackets.

Example: PALE [PART] TIRE : LAMB [**LAMP**] PUMP

93.	RISK [RICE] LACE	: LAME [ ] BEST	93. ....
94.	MATE [FARM] FROM	: LEAN [ ] MAZE	94. ....
95.	FOAM [ROOF] ROSE	: TAIL [ ] NEED	95. ....
96.	CLIMB [CALM] FARM	: SLAVE [ ] FAME	96. ....
97.	LAUGH [GALE] LEAP	: HURRY [ ] STAY	97. ....
98.	BROAD [DARE] EVERY	: INGOT [ ] TREAD	98. ....
99.	SPARE [READ] DAILY	: FLAME [ ] LORRY	99. ....
100.	TABLE [BLOW] OWNER	: REMIT [ ] CEASE	100. ....

THIS IS THE LAST PAGE

Total

✓	This page
	16

Practice Paper 2

(Verbal Reasoning)

Please read the following before you start the Practice Paper:

1.   Do not begin the Practice Paper until you are told to do so.

2.   The Practice Paper contains 100 questions and you have 50 minutes to complete it.

3.   Read the questions carefully so that you know what to do.

4.   Try and answer as many questions as you can. You may not be able to answer all of them, so if you cannot answer a question go on to the next one. Do not spend too much time on one question.

5.   Write your answers clearly. If you want to change an answer, put a single line through the wrong answer and write the correct answer clearly.

6.   When you get to the end of the Practice Paper, go back and check your answers.

In the questions below write the number in the brackets that continues the sequence.

Example: 5, 9, 13, 17, [**21**]

1.	2, 7, 12, 17, 22,	[ ]	1. ....
2.	27, 24, 21, 18, 15,	[ ]	2. ....
3.	3, 6, 12, 24,	[ ]	3. ....
4.	8, 9, 11, 14, 18, 23,	[ ]	4. ....
5.	12, 4, 14, 7, 17, 11, 21, 16,	[ ]	5. ....
6.	3, 3, 6, 18,	[ ]	6. ....
7.	64, 32, 16, 8,	[ ]	7. ....
8.	24, 11, 20, 13, 16, 15, 12,	[ ]	8. ....

Using the alphabet shown below, identify the next letters in the sequences and write them in the brackets.

A B C D E F G H I J K L M N O P Q R S T U V W X Y Z

Example: JG, LI, NK, PM, [RO]

9.	BJ,	DM,	FP,	HS,	JV,	[LW]	9. ....
10.	WN,	TQ,	QT,	NW,		[KZ]	10. ....
11.	EF,	FE,	HC,	KZ,	OV,	[SR]	11. ....
12.	BY,	DV,	GS,	KP,	PM,	[VJ]	12. ....
13.	II,	JJ,	LL,	OP,	SX,	[XG]	13. ....
14.	MA,	NZ,	LB,	OY,	KC,	PX,	[JD]	14. ....
15.	MP,	MM,	QI,	QD,	UX,	[UQ]	15. ....

PLEASE CONTINUE ON THE NEXT PAGE

✓	This page
Total	15

In the following questions underline **two** words that are **different** from the others.

Example: [screen, mouse, <u>telephone</u>, keyboard, <u>table</u>]

16. [pineapple, mango, onion, broccoli, cherry]

17. [herd, cows, flock, shoal, sheep]

18. [cod, haddock, crab, heron, mackerel]

19. [cygnet, lamb, horse, foal, pig]

20. [rock, river, boat, stream, brook]

21. [architect, nurse, doctor, surgeon, joiner]

22. [dollar, franc, kilo, peseta, yard]

In the questions below underline **two** words, one from each group, that are **opposite** in meaning.

Example: [expensive, <u>optional</u>, trust]   [<u>compulsory</u>, tight, pretend]

23. [oppose, please, blind]   [provide, shine, support]

24. [travel, find, superior]   [hurry, better, inferior]

25. [bread, seek, comic]   [serious, shop, predict]

26. [despair, quote, prefer]   [weather, racket, hope]

27. [level, fashion, main]   [produce, uneven, wash]

28. [track, supple, various]   [rigid, expire, promise]

29. [ancient, know, opaque]   [range, clear, absent]

30. [tidiness, deny, behind]   [late, delay, disorder]

23. ....
24. ....
25. ....
26. ....
27. ....
28. ....
29. ....
30. ....

PLEASE CONTINUE ON THE NEXT PAGE

✓	This page
Total	15

In the sentences below a four letter word is hidden at the end of one word and the start of the next. Write the four letter word in the brackets. You must not change the order of the letters.

Example: All the boy's journeys we<u>re ad</u>venturous.   [**read**   ]

31. She owes that money to Dad.   [   ]   31. ....

32. I hope all the children arrive.   [   ]   32. ....

33. Which boy opened the vent again?   [   ]   33. ....

34. She ate the cake before lunch.   [   ]   34. ....

35. He borrowed my ball and bat.   [   ]   35. ....

36. You have stopped before the line.   [   ]   36. ....

37. We must arrange to play again.   [   ]   37. ....

38. Daniel, Robert and Rebecca need to be able to jump 1.5 metres to join the school high jump team.
Daniel and Rebecca can both jump higher than Robert.
Robert can only jump 1.4 metres high.

Which one of the following must be true? Write your answer in the brackets.

A. None of the children join the high jump team.
B. Only Rebecca joins the high jump team.
C. Robert doesn't join the high jump team.
D. Daniel and Rebecca join the high jump team.
E. Robert is offered a place in the team but decides not to accept it.   [   ]   38. ....

39. Bruce, Fiona and Terence catch buses to go to the same destination.

Bruce catches the 11.15 am bus.
Fiona's bus journey takes twice as long as Terence's.
Fiona leaves 15 minutes before Bruce and arrives at 12.30 pm.
Terence catches the 11.45 am bus.

What time does Terence arrive at the destination?   [   ]   39. ....

✓	This page
Total	9

PLEASE CONTINUE ON THE NEXT PAGE

In the following questions numbers have been replaced with letters. Work out the answer to the sum and write this in the brackets.

Example: If A = 4, B = 3, C = 2 and D = 1, find the answer to this sum, and **write it as a number**.

A + B + D = [**8**]

40. If A = 4, B = 6, C = 8 and D = 10, find the answer to this sum, and **write it as a number**.
D + A - B = [   ]

41. If A = 5, B = 4, C = 3 and D = 2, find the answer to this sum, and **write it as a number**.
C x B x A = [   ]

42. If A = 10, B = 8, C = 6 and D = 4, find the answer to this sum, and **write it as a number**.
A x B ÷ D = [   ]

43. If A = 11, B = 8, C = 9 and D = 10, find the answer to this sum, and **write it as a number**.
D + B + C - A = [   ]

44. If A = 8, B = 6, C = 4 and D = 2, find the answer to this sum, and **write it as a number**.
A x B ÷ C ÷ D = [   ]

45. If A = 2, B = 10, C = 15 and D = 20, find the answer to this sum, and **write it as a number**.
A x B x D = [   ]

46. If A = 8, B = 5, C = 4 and D = 3, find the answer to this sum, and **write it as a number**.
A - B - D = [   ]

47. If A = 25, B = 20, C = 15 and D = 10, find the answer to this sum, and **write it as a number**.
A + B - C - D = [   ]

Please leave this column blank

40. ....

41. ....

42. ....

43. ....

44. ....

45. ....

46. ....

47. ....

PLEASE CONTINUE ON THE NEXT PAGE

	✓	This page
Total		8

In the following questions the word which has been underlined has had three consecutive letters removed. These three letters make a correctly spelt word without being rearranged. Write the three-letter word in the brackets.

Example: The manr selected the soccer team. [**age**]

#	Question	Answer
48.	The train deps from the station in one hour.	[ ]
49.	He tped over the kerb.	[ ]
50.	Two mullied by two equals four.	[ ]
51.	It's beging to rain.	[ ]
52.	He exded the ladder so that he could climb higher.	[ ]
53.	The magician made the rabbit disapp.	[ ]
54.	She read the book to increase her knowge.	[ ]

In the following questions there are two groups of words. The word in brackets on the left-hand side has been formed in a certain way using letters from the other words on the left-hand side. Use the letters in the words on the right-hand side to form a word **in the same way**. Write your answer in the brackets.

Example: RACE [FACE] FIND : LAST [**MAST**] MAIL

55.	MICE [MEAT] DATE	: PACE [ ] SALE	55. ....
56.	FARM [STAR] LAST	: LAND [ ] MALE	56. ....
57.	HOPE [PEST] STOP	: VEST [ ] ABLE	57. ....
58.	FOAL [LOAN] NAIL	: COMB [ ] TAIL	58. ....
59.	STARE [TEND] BEND	: APPLE [ ] KEEP	59. ....
60.	TOAST [RATE] REST	: CHAIR [ ] DEAF	60. ....
61.	BADGE [GEAR] RISK	: RAISE [ ] TRIP	61. ....
62.	CREAM [READ] BLAND	: BROOM [ ] STICK	62. ....

PLEASE CONTINUE ON THE NEXT PAGE

✓	This page
Total	15

In the following questions the pairs of letters are related in the same way. Use the alphabet shown below to work out the missing letters. Write the answer in the brackets.

A B C D E F G H I J K L M N O P Q R S T U V W X Y Z

Example: FG is related to HI as PQ is related to   [RS   ]

63. KN is related to MQ as AB is related to   [   ]   63. ....

64. JB is related to FF as UG is related to   [   ]   64. ....

65. XW is related to RY as GM is related to   [   ]   65. ....

66. AD is related to AF as PH is related to   [   ]   66. ....

67. MO is related to WE as CN is related to   [   ]   67. ....

68. SQ is related to WL as TR is related to   [   ]   68. ....

69. ZA is related to CX as FS is related to   [   ]   69. ....

70. NC is related to MA as RI is related to   [   ]   70. ....

In each of the following questions, underline one word from each pair of brackets that will complete the sentence in the most sensible way.

Example: Arrow is to [<u>bow</u>, line, archer] as bullet is to [shoot, <u>gun</u>, target].

71. Nose is to [knows, face, smell] as mail is to [letter, post, male].   71. ....

72. Water is to [kettle, rain, coffee] as milk is to [cow, jug, cream].   72. ....

73. Train is to [rail, station, journey] as boat is to [dock, yacht, sail].   73. ....

74. Twins is to [pair, children, pear] as triplets is to [family, triple, trio].   74. ....

75. Leveret is to [rabbit, hair, hare] as cub is to [fox, scout, sheep].   75. ....

76. Right is to [write, left, turn] as up is to [jump, stop, down].   76. ....

77. Badger is to [set, animal, owl] as robin is to [garden, nest, fly].   77. ....

	✓	This page
		15

PLEASE CONTINUE ON THE NEXT PAGE   Total

In these questions the three numbers in each group are related in exactly the same way. Calculate the number to complete the third group and write it in the brackets.

Example: (4 [6] 8)   (5 [10] 15)   (3 [**6**] 9)

78. (3 [6] 9)   (4 [8] 12)   (6 [   ] 18)
79. (48 [6] 8)   (49 [7] 7)   (63 [   ] 7)
80. (72 [47] 24)   (28 [18] 9)   (84 [   ] 33)
81. (90 [15] 9)   (66 [16] 6)   (27 [   ] 9)
82. (3 [21] 27)   (6 [25] 37)   (11 [   ] 23)
83. (22 [40] 9)   (5 [29] 12)   (16 [   ] 18)
84. (12 [50] 5)   (11 [111] 11)   (9 [   ] 9)

In the questions below underline **two** words, one from each group, that make a new word when combined. The word from the group on the left must come first.

Example: [ran, fat, press]   [hit, high, her]

85. [palm, lift, scar]   [past, disk, let]
86. [run, part, stare]   [ridge, shine, find]
87. [pop, ride, want]   [spy, pies, elf]
88. [spot, book, car]   [pet, pine, add]
89. [can, time, mist]   [list, on, farm]
90. [bark, off, skip]   [first, ice, right]
91. [slit, key, write]   [tread, spin, her]
92. [aged, flour, spar]   [row, risk, slide]

Please leave this column blank

78. ....
79. ....
80. ....
81. ....
82. ....
83. ....
84. ....

85. ....
86. ....
87. ....
88. ....
89. ....
90. ....
91. ....
92. ....

PLEASE CONTINUE ON THE NEXT PAGE

✓	This page
Total	15

In the following questions some of the words have been written in code. In each question the code has been "broken" for one word. You must use the same code to work out the second word and write the answer in the brackets.

The alphabet has been printed to help you.

A B C D E F G H I J K L M N O P Q R S T U V W X Y Z

Example: If SHLD means TIME, what does RSNO mean? [STOP]

93. If WFNI is the code for RAID,
what is the code for LIST? [ ] 93. ....

94. If RYZJC means TABLE,
what does FMSQC mean? [ ] 94. ....

95. If YTKUV is the code for WRIST,
what is the code for SPACE? [ ] 95. ....

96. If MKJLY is the code for LIGHT,
what is the code for SLIME? [ ] 96. ....

97. If QBACHU means RABBIT,
what does FFQCHM mean? [ ] 97. ....

98. If UFLTUS is the code for SCHOOL,
what is the code for PENCIL? [ ] 98. ....

99. If SQKFI is the code for SPICE,
what is the code for HASTE? [ ] 99. ....

100. If QLYSA means SPEAK,
what does NWMLQ mean? [ ] 100. ....

THIS IS THE LAST PAGE

	This page
✓	
Total	8

Practice Paper 3

(Verbal Reasoning)

Please complete these details before you begin:

Date: ....

Your Name: ....

Date of Birth: ....

School: ....

Please read the following before you start the Practice Paper:

1. Do not begin the Practice Paper until you are told to do so.

2. The Practice Paper contains 100 questions and you have 50 minutes to complete it.

3. Read the questions carefully so that you know what to do.

4. Try and answer as many questions as you can. You may not be able to answer all of them, so if you cannot answer a question go on to the next one. Do not spend too much time on one question.

5. Write your answers clearly. If you want to change an answer, put a single line through the wrong answer and write the correct answer clearly.

6. When you get to the end of the Practice Paper, go back and check your answers.

In each of the following questions, underline one word from each pair of brackets that will complete the sentence in the most sensible way.

Example: Ash is to [<u>tree</u>, fire, smoke] as tulip is to [<u>flower</u>, Spring, crocus].

1. West is to [East, compass, North] as left is to [leave, write, right].

2. Weigh is to [scales, way, heavy] as sight is to [site, see, bright].

3. Tallest is to [shortest, maximum, biggest] as oldest is to [old, ancient, youngest].

4. Paris is to [Belgium, Nice, France] as Brussels is to [sprout, Belgium, Italy].

5. Nest is to [tree, home, bird] as hive is to [honey, bee, be].

6. Book is to [read, page, magazine] as ruler is to [measure, metre, king].

7. Cow is to [milk, bull, farm] as goose is to [gander, geese, bird].

1. ....
2. ....
3. ....
4. ....
5. ....
6. ....
7. ....

In the questions below there are two sets of words. Find a word that goes equally well with both sets and write this in the brackets.

Example: [dish, basin]   [roll, throw]   [**bowl**]

8. [pole, mast]   [mail, letters]   [   ]

9. [earth, land]   [crushed, smoothed]   [   ]

10. [arrow, missile]   [dash, hasten]   [   ]

11. [follow, hunt]   [twig, stem]   [   ]

12. [escape, flee]   [lock, fasten]   [   ]

13. [shoreline, beach]   [freewheel, cruise]   [   ]

14. [feed, eat]   [gouge, scrape]   [   ]

15. [fixed, constant]   [shelter, stall]   [   ]

8. ....
9. ....
10. ....
11. ....
12. ....
13. ....
14. ....
15. ....

PLEASE CONTINUE ON THE NEXT PAGE

Total

✓	This page
	15

In the sentences below a four letter word is hidden at the end of one word and the start of the next word. Write the four letter word in the brackets. You must not change the order of the letters.

Example: Please can we lis<u>ten t</u>o music?   [**tent**   ]

16. The brush belonged to the artist.   [   ]   16. ....

17. Should I close all the windows?   [   ]   17. ....

18. Did the cow enter the field?   [   ]   18. ....

19. The bride arrived at the church.   [   ]   19. ....

20. You are not allowed to talk.   [   ]   20. ....

21. This piano seems out of tune.   [   ]   21. ....

22. The hamster managed to escape again.   [   ]   22. ....

In the questions below underline **two** words, one from each group, that are **similar** in meaning.

Example: [<u>real</u>, pretend, unsure]   [<u>actual</u>, relax, ready]

23. [emit, donor, dormant]   [asleep, roam, tension]   23. ....

24. [sturdy, annoy, doubt]   [rule, solid, nimble]   24. ....

25. [spacious, drag, kind]   [night, haul, success]   25. ....

26. [reduce, alert, pretend]   [dismiss, stage, decrease]   26. ....

27. [stern, bend, attack]   [stoop, happy, desperate]   27. ....

28. [wither, enormous, join]   [connect, angular, treat]   28. ....

29. [ordinary, tender, tidy]   [tolerate, neat, expensive]   29. ....

30. [vicious, wild, shout]   [straight, exclaim, march]   30. ....

PLEASE CONTINUE ON THE NEXT PAGE

Total

✓	This page
	15

In the following questions the word which has been underlined has had three consecutive letters removed. These three letters make a correctly spelt word without being rearranged. Write the three-letter word in the brackets.

Example: The robber <u>sted</u> the car and then drove off. [**art**]

31. The jewels <u>glised</u> in the sunlight. [ ] 31. ....

32. My Dad won't <u>al</u> me to go to the party. [ ] 32. ....

33. The girl swam <u>tods</u> the shore. [ ] 33. ....

34. What's the difference between an alligator and a <u>croile</u>? [ ] 34. ....

35. The referee reached for his <u>wtle</u>. [ ] 35. ....

36. She promised to call me on the <u>teleph</u>. [ ] 36. ....

37. The lady put the <u>fers</u> in the vase. [ ] 37. ....

In the questions below you must move one letter from the word on the left to the word on the right to make two new words. You are only allowed to move one letter and must not re-arrange any of the other letters. Write both new words in the brackets.

Example:
CAMEL   AIR   [**Came**]   [**Lair**]

38. YEAST   DEN   [ ]   [ ] 38. ....

39. CLIMB   RATE   [ ]   [ ] 39. ....

40. CRAVE   ICE   [ ]   [ ] 40. ....

41. BLOWN   KNOW   [ ]   [ ] 41. ....

42. RIDGE   EAR   [ ]   [ ] 42. ....

43. HERON   CROW   [ ]   [ ] 43. ....

44. GRAIN   ROD   [ ]   [ ] 44. ....

PLEASE CONTINUE ON THE NEXT PAGE

Total

✓	This page
	14

In the following questions, numbers have been replaced with letters. Work out the answer to the sum and write this in the brackets.

Example: If A = 6, B = 4, C = 2 and D = 1, find the answer to this sum, and **write it as a number**.

A + B + D = [**11**]

45.   If A = 4, B = 3, C = 2 and D = 1, find the answer to this sum, and **write it as a number**.

A - B + D = [   ]

45.   ....

46.   If A = 2, B = 4, C = 6 and D = 8, find the answer to this sum, and **write it as a number**.

D ÷ A x B = [   ]

46.   ....

47.   If A = 10, B = 5, C = 4 and D = 3, find the answer to this sum, and **write it as a number**.

A + B - C - D = [   ]

47.   ....

48.   If A = 3, B = 4, C = 5 and D = 6, find the answer to this sum, and **write it as a number**.

A x B x D = [   ]

48.   ....

49.   If A = 20, B = 15, C = 10 and D = 5, find the answer to this sum, and **write it as a number**.

A - B - D + C = [   ]

49.   ....

50.   If A = 6, B = 4, C = 10 and D = 20, find the answer to this sum, and **write it as a number**.

A x B x C = [   ]

50.   ....

51.   If A = 5, B = 10, C = 25 and D = 50, find the answer to this sum, and **write it as a number**.

D ÷ B ÷ A = [   ]

51.   ....

52.   If A = 4, B = 8, C = 12 and D = 16, find the answer to this sum, and **write it as a number**.

B ÷ A x D = [   ]

52.   ....

PLEASE CONTINUE ON THE NEXT PAGE

	✓	This page
Total		8

There are four words and three codes written below. The codes are in a different order to the words and one code is missing.

STEM   FEAR   MATE   PART

    2791   6713   4379

Write the answer to the questions below in the brackets.

53.   What is the code number for MARE?   [   ]   53. ....

54.   Which word has the code number 19371?   [   ]   54. ....

55.   What is the code number for PEAR?   [   ]   55. ....

56.   Which word has the code number 1791?   [   ]   56. ....

57.   What is the code number for TRAP?   [   ]   57. ....

58.   Which word has the code number 479639?   [   ]   58. ....

59.   What is the code number for FEAT?   [   ]   59. ....

---

60.   Peter, Danielle, Simon, Nirmal and Steven all play in a soccer team.
Last season they scored 11, 10, 7, 6 and 6 goals, but not in this order.
Peter scored one more goal than Nirmal.
Simon scored one more goal than Steven.
Danielle scored fewer goals than Nirmal.

Which 2 players scored the fewest goals?   [   ] [   ]   60. ....

---

61.   X, Y and Z are aeroplanes that fly from London to New York.

X leaves London at 11.30 am.
Y takes twice as long as Z to fly to New York.
Y leaves 30 minutes after X and arrives at 8.00 pm.
Z leaves at 11.45 am.

What time does Z land at New York?   [   ]   61. ....

PLEASE CONTINUE ON THE NEXT PAGE

Total   ✓   This page   9

In the following questions underline **two** words that are **different** from the others.

Example: [Mars, Saturn, <u>rocket</u>, Moon, <u>sky</u>]

62. [eagle, osprey, robin, kestrel, sparrow]

63. [leaf, branch, bird, root, squirrel]

64. [pen, chalk, pencil, paper, book]

65. [tulip, flower, crocus, daffodil, sycamore]

66. [Thames, London, Manchester, Mersey, Nile]

67. [drake, ram, ewe, cow, bull]

62.	....
63.	....
64.	....
65.	....
66.	....
67.	....

In the following questions the pairs of letters are related in the same way. Use the alphabet shown below to work out the missing letters. Write the answer in the brackets.

A B C D E F G H I J K L M N O P Q R S T U V W X Y Z

Example: DE is related to FH as NL is related to [PO]

68. QA is related to NG as FG is related to [   ]

69. JR is related to FM as ZO is related to [   ]

70. ZX is related to TB as YY is related to [   ]

71. KR is related to NN as QF is related to [   ]

72. JM is related to OS as MF is related to [   ]

73. FB is related to DE as IU is related to [   ]

74. FW is related to FG as HS is related to [   ]

75. YC is related to TY as WY is related to [   ]

68.	....
69.	....
70.	....
71.	....
72.	....
73.	....
74.	....
75.	....

PLEASE CONTINUE ON THE NEXT PAGE

	✓	This page
Total		14

Practice Paper 3, Page 6

In the following questions some of the words have been written in code. In each question the code has been "broken" for one word. You must use the same code to work out the second word and write the answer in the brackets.

The alphabet has been printed to help you.

A B C D E F G H I J K L M N O P Q R S T U V W X Y Z

Example: If QBJS means PAIR, what does LJOE mean?   [KIND   ]

76.   If UVQR is the code for STOP,
      what is the code for LINK?   [   ]

77.   If EXMMV means HAPPY,
      what does AOFSB mean?   [   ]

78.   If UWNEJ means PRIZE,
      what does GWJFI mean?   [   ]

79.   If QRYZJC means STABLE,
      what does FMPQCQ mean?   [   ]

80.   If NUROJGE is the code for HOLIDAY,
      what is the code for WINDOW?   [   ]

81.   If TQJEFS is the code for SPIDER,
      what is the code for COBWEB?   [   ]

82.   If NWLLO means PARTY,
      what does AKOFJ mean?   [   ]

83.   If XQJSF is the code for WRITE,
      what is the code for PRINT?   [   ]

84.   If DYULJN means CARPET,
      what does TRUESA mean?   [   ]

76.	....
77.	....
78.	....
79.	....
80.	....
81.	....
82.	....
83.	....
84.	....

Please leave this column blank

PLEASE CONTINUE ON THE NEXT PAGE

Total

✓	This page
	9

In the following questions there are two groups of words. The word in brackets on the left-hand side has been formed in a certain way using letters from the other words on the left-hand side. Use the letters in the words on the right-hand side to form a word **in the same way**. Write your answer in the brackets.

Example: GOLF [LOAF] PALE : ROPE [POLE] PLOD

85.	PLANT [LAMP] PALM	:	SLIME [ ] TIES	85. ....
86.	PRINT [RING] GALE	:	SWING [ ] DAZE	86. ....
87.	RISK [RARE] AREA	:	EAST [ ] POND	87. ....
88.	FRAME [RAMP] STOP	:	CLIFF [ ] PLOT	88. ....
89.	TASTE [MAST] AIMS	:	PRIZE [ ] LOST	89. ....
90.	PLANT [LANE] ROSES	:	PRISM [ ] KICKS	90. ....
91.	GIFT [FAIR] RATE	:	TACK [ ] TONE	91. ....
92.	SHOP [FISH] FIND	:	STEP [ ] LONG	92. ....

In the questions below write the number in the brackets that continues the sequence.

Example: 5, 10, 15, 20, [25]

93.	4, 9, 14, 19, 24,	[ ]	93. ....
94.	19, 17, 15, 13, 11,	[ ]	94. ....
95.	2, 3, 4, 6, 6, 9, 8,	[ ]	95. ....
96.	21, 20, 18, 15, 15, 10,	[ ]	96. ....
97.	15, 15, 16, 14, 17, 13, 18,	[ ]	97. ....
98.	16, 14, 18, 12, 20, 10,	[ ]	98. ....
99.	9, 8, 18, 16, 27, 24,	[ ]	99. ....
100.	17, 4, 15, 8, 13, 12,	[ ]	100. ....

THIS IS THE LAST PAGE

	√	This page
Total		16

Practice Paper 4

(Verbal Reasoning)

Please complete these details before you begin:

Date: ....

Your Name: ....

Date of Birth: ....

School: ....

Please read the following before you start the Practice Paper:

1. Do not begin the Practice Paper until you are told to do so.

2. The Practice Paper contains 100 questions and you have 50 minutes to complete it.

3. Read the questions carefully so that you know what to do.

4. Try and answer as many questions as you can. You may not be able to answer all of them, so if you cannot answer a question go on to the next one. Do not spend too much time on one question.

5. Write your answers clearly. If you want to change an answer, put a single line through the wrong answer and write the correct answer clearly.

6. When you get to the end of the Practice Paper, go back and check your answers.

In these questions the three numbers in each group are related in exactly the same way. Calculate the number to complete the third group and write it in the brackets.

Example: (2 [4] 6)   (11 [13] 15)   (9 [**11**] 13)

1.   (24 [16] 8)   (32 [24] 8)   (25 [   ] 15)

2.   (4 [60] 15)   (9 [54] 6)   (11 [   ] 6)

3.   (27 [17] 8)   (18 [4] 12)   (34 [   ] 8)

4.   (88 [15] 8)   (45 [9] 9)   (18 [   ] 2)

5.   (16 [40] 12)   (7 [21] 7)   (4 [   ] 19)

6.   (24 [2] 6)   (20 [1] 10)   (30 [   ] 15)

7.   (17 [35] 2)   (6 [37] 6)   (6 [   ] 7)

Please leave this column blank

1. ....
2. ....
3. ....
4. ....
5. ....
6. ....
7. ....

In the following questions there are two groups of words. The word in brackets on the left-hand side has been formed in a certain way using letters from the other words on the left-hand side. Use the letters in the words on the right-hand side to form a word **in the same way**. Write your answer in the brackets.

Example: BONY [TINY] TICK : LOST [**FAST**] FARM

8.   CART [PART] PLUM   :   GOLD [   ] FUSS

9.   MAIL [LION] MOON   :   BEAM [   ] CORE

10.   LOBE [BOAT] TEAR   :   POND [   ] EASY

11.   MAZE [LEAP] POLE   :   AREA [   ] TAPS

12.   HOLLY [SHOE] SEAT   :   AFTER [   ] SEAM

13.   CROAK [CASH] SHOAL   :   MONEY [   ] ANGER

14.   LARGE [MALE] TRAMP   :   LADLE [   ] SPADE

15.   PLATE [TAME] BEAM   :   PLACE [   ] BEAK

8. ....
9. ....
10. ....
11. ....
12. ....
13. ....
14. ....
15. ....

PLEASE CONTINUE ON THE NEXT PAGE

√ | This page
Total | 15

In the following questions, numbers have been replaced with letters. Work out the answer to the sum and write this in the brackets.

Example: If A = 10, B = 8, C = 6 and D = 4, find the answer to this sum, and **write it as a number**.

A - C + D = [**8**]

16. If A = 6, B = 5, C = 4 and D = 2, find the answer to this sum, and **write it as a number**.

A ÷ D x B = [   ]

17. If A = 5, B = 4, C = 3 and D = 2, find the answer to this sum, and **write it as a number**.

A x B x D = [   ]

18. If A = 2, B = 3, C = 4 and D = 5, find the answer to this sum, and **write it as a number**.

A x B x C x D = [   ]

19. If A = 10, B = 9, C = 8 and D = 7, find the answer to this sum, and **write it as a number**.

A + B + C - D = [   ]

20. If A = 20, B = 15, C = 10 and D = 5, find the answer to this sum, and **write it as a number**.

A x C ÷ D = [   ]

21. If A = 8, B = 6, C = 4 and D = 2, find the answer to this sum, and **write it as a number**.

C x D ÷ A = [   ]

22. If A = 10, B = 15, C = 20 and D = 25, find the answer to this sum, and **write it as a number**.

A + B + C - D = [   ]

23. If A = 2, B = 4, C = 6 and D = 8, find the answer to this sum, and **write it as a number**.

A x B x C ÷ D = [   ]

Please leave this column blank
16. ....
17. ....
18. ....
19. ....
20. ....
21. ....
22. ....
23. ....

PLEASE CONTINUE ON THE NEXT PAGE

Total

✓	This page
	8

In the questions below write the number in the brackets that continues the sequence.

Example: 6, 11, 16, 21, [**26**]

24. 18, 15, 12, 9, 6,   [   ]   24. ....

25. 5, 7, 10, 14, 19,   [   ]   25. ....

26. 25, 21, 18, 16,   [   ]   26. ....

27. 2, 4, 8, 16,   [   ]   27. ....

28. 8, 9, 10, 7, 12, 5, 14,   [   ]   28. ....

29. 20, 32, 15, 16, 10, 8,   [   ]   29. ....

30. 19, 2, 14, 4, 10, 6, 7, 8,   [   ]   30. ....

31. 26, 13, 22, 15, 18, 17,   [   ]   31. ....

32.   Tracey, Antonio and Douglas need to be able to cycle 1 km in less than 4 minutes to join the local cycling club.

Douglas and Antonio can both cycle 1 km more quickly than Tracey.

It takes Tracey 5 minutes to cycle 1 km.

Which one of the following must be true? Write your answer in the brackets.

A. Only Antonio is offered a place in the cycling club.
B. Tracey doesn't join the cycling club.
C. Douglas and Antonio join the cycling club.
D. Tracey and Antonio don't join the cycling club.
E. Only Douglas joins the cycling club.   [   ]   32. ....

✓	This page
Total	9

PLEASE CONTINUE ON THE NEXT PAGE

In the following questions, calculate the number that will complete the sum and put your answer in the brackets.

		Please leave this column blank

Example: 7 + 12 = 14 + ?   [5   ]

33. 54 + 19 - 7 = 20 x 3 + ?   [   ]   33. ....

34. 6 x 8 - 4 = 5 + 30 + ?   [   ]   34. ....

35. 7 x 6 ÷ 2 = 30 + 4 - ?   [   ]   35. ....

36. 19 x 2 + 8 = 2 x 8 + ?   [   ]   36. ....

37. 108 ÷ 36 x 8 = 2 x 6 x ?   [   ]   37. ....

38. 6 x 14 - 28 = 7 x 6 + ?   [   ]   38. ....

39. 54 ÷ 18 + 12 = 6 x 4 - ?   [   ]   39. ....

Using the alphabet shown below, identify the next letters in the sequences and write them in the brackets.

A B C D E F G H I J K L M N O P Q R S T U V W X Y Z

Example: CR, EQ, GP, IO, [KN]

40. DR,   FP,   HN,   JL,   [   ]   40. ....

41. HR,   EV,   BZ,   YD,   [   ]   41. ....

42. BL,   CJ,   EH,   HF,   [   ]   42. ....

43. NV,   PS,   TP,   VM,   ZJ,   [   ]   43. ....

44. JP,   MS,   GP,   PS,   [   ]   44. ....

45. NC,   PF,   MJ,   QO,   [   ]   45. ....

46. OW,   RT,   MN,   TE,   [   ]   46. ....

PLEASE CONTINUE ON THE NEXT PAGE

✓	This page
Total	14

In the following questions underline **two** words that are **different** from the others.

Example: [tea, lemonade, <u>drink</u>, <u>cup</u>, coffee]

47. [school, teacher, university, pupil, college]   47. ....

48. [Spanish, French, Germany, Italian, European]   48. ....

49. [leaf, dandelion, flower, pansy, sweetpea]   49. ....

50. [glider, car, van, train, aeroplane]   50. ....

51. [crocodile, frog, lion, newt, mouse]   51. ....

52. [centimetre, measure, foot, yard, acre]   52. ....

53. [triangle, circle, oval, pentagon, square]   53. ....

In the questions below underline **two** words, one from each group, that are **opposite** in meaning.

Example: [<u>cold</u>, bright, catch]   [plod, quickly, <u>hot</u>]

54. [hollow, shrewd, steadily]   [ancient, stupid, serpent]   54. ....

55. [glum, shop, critic]   [cheerful, collapse, frighten]   55. ....

56. [comfortable, cold, combine]   [demand, examination, disperse]   56. ....

57. [courageous, happy, commit]   [creation, music, cowardly]   57. ....

58. [tidy, create, pleasant]   [deny, destroy, new]   58. ....

59. [glossy, coax, praise]   [current, dull, extinct]   59. ....

60. [chart, rumour, allow]   [support, prohibit, trespass]   60. ....

61. [wriggle, partition, true]   [start, exterior, inaccurate]   61. ....

✓	This page
	15

PLEASE CONTINUE ON THE NEXT PAGE   Total

In the following questions some of the words have been written in code. In each question the code has been "broken" for one word. You must use the same code to work out the second word and write the answer in the brackets.

The alphabet has been printed to help you.

A B C D E F G H I J K L M N O P Q R S T U V W X Y Z

Example: If EQNF means COLD, what does TWUV mean? [RUST]

62. If MIXV is the code for PLAY,
    what is the code for DISH? [AFPE]

63. If CCUO means BARK,
    what does HQOH mean? [GOLD]

64. If KCFCA is the code for MAIZE,
    what is the code for WHEAT? [UJBDP]

65. If MRABR means SWEET,
    what does WVJAW mean? [CANDY]

66. If NPGAC means PRICE,
    what does FYNNW mean? [HAPPY]

67. If UXUDO is the code for STOVE,
    what is the code for PLACE? [RPGKO]

68. If UFYBU means RIVER,
    what does EORLN mean? [BROOK]

69. If QLYSA is the code for PENCE,
    what is the code for POUND? [QVFDZ]

70. Deborah, Kevin, Jennifer, Annabelle and Bernard are all in a cross-country running team.
    Deborah goes running on Tuesdays and Thursdays.
    Kevin, Annabelle and Bernard go running on Mondays, Tuesdays and Fridays.
    Jennifer goes running on Mondays, Wednesdays and Saturdays. On Saturdays she goes running with Annabelle.
    Everyone in the team except Bernard go running on Sundays.

    Who goes running most often? [Annabelle]

PLEASE CONTINUE ON THE NEXT PAGE

✓	This page
Total	9

In the questions below you must move one letter from the word on the left to the word on the right to make two new words. You are only allowed to move one letter and must not re-arrange any of the other letters. Write both new words in the brackets.

Example:

RAPID	MALE	[Raid]	[Maple]	

71.	PLEAD	RAISE	[　　　]	[　　　]	71. ....
72.	PLANT	ALE	[　　　]	[　　　]	72. ....
73.	CHAIR	LOCK	[　　　]	[　　　]	73. ....
74.	CARVE	STARE	[　　　]	[　　　]	74. ....
75.	BRING	ROOM	[　　　]	[　　　]	75. ....
76.	ERASE	DAFT	[　　　]	[　　　]	76. ....
77.	FALLOW	EEL	[　　　]	[　　　]	77. ....

In the questions below underline **two** words, one from each group, that make a new word when combined. The word from the group on the left must come first.

Example: [<u>assist</u>, hole, fight]　　[term, pine, <u>ant</u>]

78.	[tar, far, par]	[thing, den, most]	78. ....
79.	[cash, near, gold]	[sold, rage, mere]	79. ....
80.	[tap, high, find]	[send, rope, way]	80. ....
81.	[spot, disc, wool]	[silk, lime, lens]	81. ....
82.	[up, shine, in]	[down, vest, calm]	82. ....
83.	[out, side, slow]	[rage, part, inner]	83. ....
84.	[book, gear, wait]	[stem, tin, box]	84. ....
85.	[back, flow, croak]	[list, dog, ward]	85. ....

PLEASE CONTINUE ON THE NEXT PAGE

	✓	This page
Total		15

In the following questions the pairs of letters are related in the same way. Use the alphabet shown below to work out the missing letters. Write the answer in the brackets.

A B C D E F G H I J K L M N O P Q R S T U V W X Y Z

Example: QV is related to ST as FJ is related to [**HH**]

86. JA is related to ME as AV is related to [DZ]

87. GB is related to BB as NS is related to [IS]

88. RX is related to OA as EL is related to [BO]

89. XX is related to VT as MO is related to [KK]

90. GA is related to BW as KR is related to [FN]

91. PC is related to ZH as SY is related to [CD]

92. QY is related to NS as RL is related to [OF]

93. NF is related to FN as JJ is related to [JJ]

86.	....
87.	....
88.	....
89.	....
90.	....
91.	....
92.	....
93.	....

In each of the following questions, underline one word from each pair of brackets that will complete the sentence in the most sensible way.

Example: Calf is to [milk, farm, <u>cow</u>] as kitten is to [<u>cat</u>, dog, pet].

94. Train is to [station, carriage, track] as car is to [driver, road, engine].

95. Nose is to [face, smell, knows] as write is to [right, pencil, writer].

96. Pitch is to [football, throw, black] as court is to [judge, yard, tennis].

97. Trio is to [three, play, concert] as duo is to [double, too, two].

98. Honey is to [marmalade, bread, bee] as milk is to [bottle, cow, cream].

99. Fast is to [slow, quick, rapid] as huge is to [dinosaur, last, tiny].

100. Wait is to [waited, weight, waiting] as hurry is to [fast, slowly, hurried].

94.	....
95.	....
96.	....
97.	....
98.	....
99.	....
100.	....

THIS IS THE LAST PAGE

Total

✓	This page
	15

Practice Paper 5

(Verbal Reasoning)

Please complete these details before you begin:

Date: ....

Your Name: ....

Date of Birth: ....

School: ....

Please read the following before you start the Practice Paper:

1. Do not begin the Practice Paper until you are told to do so.

2. The Practice Paper contains 100 questions and you have 50 minutes to complete it.

3. Read the questions carefully so that you know what to do.

4. Try and answer as many questions as you can. You may not be able to answer all of them, so if you cannot answer a question go on to the next one. Do not spend too much time on one question.

5. Write your answers clearly. If you want to change an answer, put a single line through the wrong answer and write the correct answer clearly.

6. When you get to the end of the Practice Paper, go back and check your answers.

Using the alphabet shown below, identify the next letters in the sequences and write them in the brackets.

A B C D E F G H I J K L M N O P Q R S T U V W X Y Z

Example: JZ, KY, LX, MW, [NV]

1. BW, EV, HU, KT,   [   ]   1. ....

2. YD, WA, UX, SU,   [   ]   2. ....

3. AW, ET, IQ, MN,   [   ]   3. ....

4. KK, LI, NG, QE, UC,   [   ]   4. ....

5. YZ, WY, SW, MT,   [   ]   5. ....

6. EQ, HR, LP, QS, WO,   [   ]   6. ....

7. LF, MH, KL, NR, JZ,   [   ]   7. ....

---

8. Jimmy, Peter, David, Rebecca and Jenny all play tennis.
Jimmy and Jenny play tennis together on Wednesdays.
Peter, Jenny, David and Rebecca play tennis every Saturday and Monday.
Rebecca plays tennis with her sister on Tuesdays.
Jenny and David play tennis on Sundays.

Who plays tennis most often?   [   ]   8. ....

---

9. Robert, Katie and Pedro want to join the local swimming club.
To join the team you must be able to swim 200 metres.
Pedro can swim 175 metres.
Both Robert and Katie can swim further than Pedro.

Which of the following must be true? Write your answer in the brackets.

A. Robert can swim further than Katie.
B. Robert and Katie can join the swimming club.
C. Katie can swim further than Robert.
D. Pedro can't join the swimming club.
E. Only Katie is offered a place in the swimming club.   [   ]   9. ....

✓	This page
Total	9

PLEASE CONTINUE ON THE NEXT PAGE

In the following questions the word which has been underlined has had three consecutive letters removed. These three letters make a correctly spelt word without being rearranged. Write the three-letter word in the brackets.

Example: The elephant picked up the log with its <u>tk</u>.   [**run**]

10.	Who is <u>ryring</u> the bag?	[ ]	10.	....
11.	I need an ink <u>cartge</u> for my pen.	[ ]	11.	....
12.	He could hear the <u>teleph</u> ringing in the next room.	[ ]	12.	....
13.	The window <u>stered</u> when the stone hit it.	[ ]	13.	....
14.	The chef put some <u>tomas</u> in the salad.	[ ]	14.	....
15.	Is it true that most rabbits like <u>cars</u>?	[ ]	15.	....
16.	I'm going into the <u>gar</u> to mow the lawn.	[ ]	16.	....
17.	She keeps a <u>ster</u> as a pet.	[ ]	17.	....

In the sentences below a four letter word is hidden at the end of one word and the start of the next. Write the four letter word in the brackets. You must not change the order of the letters.

Example: The new vet <u>asked</u> for directions.   [**task**]

18.	The pirate started to bury treasure.	[ ]	18.	....
19.	I'll go cycling after my lunch.	[ ]	19.	....
20.	Children take ages to get ready.	[ ]	20.	....
21.	This cake is for the party.	[ ]	21.	....
22.	The aeroplane started to take-off.	[ ]	22.	....
23.	The owl and hawk are birds.	[ ]	23.	....
24.	Have you seen this old book?	[ ]	24.	....

PLEASE CONTINUE ON THE NEXT PAGE

	✓	This page
Total		15

In the questions below you must move one letter from the word on the left to the word on the right to make two new words. You are only allowed to move one letter and must not re-arrange any of the other letters. Write both new words in the brackets.

Example:

WHEAT   HEEL   [Heat   ]   [Wheel   ]

25.	BEACH	READ	[ ]	[ ]	25. ....
26.	TABLE	RIP	[ ]	[ ]	26. ....
27.	WAITER	MAD	[ ]	[ ]	27. ....
28.	PLANE	VENT	[ ]	[ ]	28. ....
29.	MARROW	ALE	[ ]	[ ]	29. ....
30.	FRAME	FIGHT	[ ]	[ ]	30. ....
31.	FLOWER	RAT	[ ]	[ ]	31. ....

In each of the following questions, underline one word from each pair of brackets that will complete the sentence in the most sensible way.

Example: Cherry is to [red, pie, <u>fruit</u>] as beech is to [sea, <u>tree</u>, sand].

32. Driver is to [bus, road, pedestrian] as astronaut is to [Mars, launch, rocket].   32.   ....

33. Bat is to [sport, hockey, cricket] as club is to [golf, tennis, skiing].   33.   ....

34. Teacher is to [school, teach, lesson] as nurse is to [doctor, patient, hospital].   34.   ....

35. Minimum is to [small, maximum, short] as fastest is to [rapid, slowest, speed].   35.   ....

36. Hammer is to [nail, screw, bolt] as saw is to [cut, wood, tools].   36.   ....

37. Pride is to [proud, horse, lion] as shoal is to [water, fish, clothing].   37.   ....

38. Right is to [wrong, letter, write] as win is to [lose, compete, race].   38.   ....

39. Find is to [seek, stop, found] as laugh is to [laughed, joke, happy].   39.   ....

✓	This page
Total	15

PLEASE CONTINUE ON THE NEXT PAGE

In the following questions the pairs of letters are related in the same way. Use the alphabet shown below to work out the missing letters. Write the answer in the brackets.

A B C D E F G H I J K L M N O P Q R S T U V W X Y Z

Example: AB is related to CD as MN is related to [OP   ]

40. CX is related to EV as UF is related to   [   ]   40.   ....

41. MQ is related to RR as CF is related to   [   ]   41.   ....

42. PS is related to MQ as GZ is related to   [   ]   42.   ....

43. WV is related to AZ as YZ is related to   [   ]   43.   ....

44. KL is related to PG as AQ is related to   [   ]   44.   ....

45. ON is related to QH as TO is related to   [   ]   45.   ....

46. NP is related to JT as ZY is related to   [   ]   46.   ....

47. NL is related to LM as QB is related to   [   ]   47.   ....

In the following questions underline **two** words that are **different** from the others.

48. [lion, pig, cow, sheep, monkey]   48.   ....

49. [car, train, bus, lorry, aeroplane]   49.   ....

50. [Paris, London, Belgium, France, Italy]   50.   ....

51. [spanner, screwdriver, nut, hammer, bolt]   51.   ....

52. [oak, beech, leaf, root, elm]   52.   ....

53. [cereal, corn, wheat, oats, potatoes]   53.   ....

54. [yacht, galleon, sailor, captain, dinghy]   54.   ....

	✓	This page
Total		15

PLEASE CONTINUE ON THE NEXT PAGE

In the questions below the **same** letter comes at the end of one word and the start of the other. The **same** letter must fit in both sets of brackets. Find the letter and write this in the brackets.

Example: rai [N] ear   bar [N] ewt

55.	lam [ ] ase	clu [ ] eat	55. ....
56.	coa [ ] ove	bow [ ] ard	56. ....
57.	dis [ ] ome	rus [ ] eat	57. ....
58.	boo [ ] iss	roo [ ] ice	58. ....
59.	fou [ ] ear	sta [ ] aid	59. ....
60.	bab [ ] ear	sta [ ] arn	60. ....
61.	tri [ ] art	har [ ] ole	61. ....
62.	roo [ ] iss	tal [ ] ite	62. ....

In the questions below underline **two** words, one from each group, that make a new word when combined. The word from the group on the left must come first.

Example: [last, <u>pass</u>, wine]   [hold, loan, <u>port</u>]

63.	[plug, wipe, coo]	[roam, pine, king]	63. ....
64.	[first, tea, poll]	[wish, ring, fold]	64. ....
65.	[stay, clock, break]	[fast, list, spin]	65. ....
66.	[arc, but, his]	[not, her, now]	66. ....
67.	[able, deny, with]	[out, part, slat]	67. ....
68.	[under, pull, spot]	[pies, over, shop]	68. ....
69.	[gate, time, he]	[art, door, copy]	69. ....
70.	[over, find, stile]	[log, pen, look]	70. ....

Please leave this column blank

✓	This page
Total	16

PLEASE CONTINUE ON THE NEXT PAGE

In the questions below underline **two** words, one from each group, that are **similar** in meaning.

Example: [<u>precious</u>, glare, stage]   [<u>valuable</u>, decide, globe]

71.	[starve, ancient, herald]	[dial, old, forest]	71.	....
72.	[deny, create, often]	[frequent, issue, trust]	72.	....
73.	[wreck, confident, tasty]	[quote, optimistic, radical]	73.	....
74.	[replica, wasted, hasten]	[draught, fasten, copy]	74.	....
75.	[fulfil, provide, sombre]	[fold, dismal, light]	75.	....
76.	[worry, fault, sledge]	[fight, tour, defect]	76.	....
77.	[pride, wise, craft]	[astute, heard, offer]	77.	....
78.	[sound, splash, ogre]	[brown, animal, secure]	78.	....

In the following questions calculate the number that will complete the sum and put your answer in the brackets.

Example: 6 + 4 = 2 + ?   [**8**]

79.	$5 \times 4 \div 2 = 7 \times 4 - ?$	[ ]	79.	....
80.	$19 - 3 + 7 = 28 + 4 - ?$	[ ]	80.	....
81.	$15 \times 5 = 3 \times 18 + ?$	[ ]	81.	....
82.	$42 \div 14 + 18 = 60 \div 3 + ?$	[ ]	82.	....
83.	$25 \times 4 - 80 = 8 \times 5 \div ?$	[ ]	83.	....
84.	$95 \div 5 - 9 = 2 \times 9 - ?$	[ ]	84.	....
85.	$144 \div 12 + 12 = 4 \times 3 \times ?$	[ ]	85.	....
86.	$120 \div 5 \div 3 = 16 \times 2 \div ?$	[ ]	86.	....

	✓	This page
Total		16

PLEASE CONTINUE ON THE NEXT PAGE

In the questions below write the number in the brackets that continues the sequence.

Example: 9, 12, 15, 18, [**21**]

87.   7, 11, 15, 19,   [   ]

88.   19, 16, 13, 10,   [   ]

89.   4, 8, 16, 32,   [   ]

90.   4, 9, 8, 14, 12, 19,   [   ]

91.   13, 5, 14, 7, 16, 10, 19, 14,   [   ]

92.   12, 3, 9, 6, 6, 9,   [   ]

93.   21, 21, 22, 19, 24, 17,   [   ]

87.	....
88.	....
89.	....
90.	....
91.	....
92.	....
93.	....

Please leave this column blank

In these questions the three numbers in each group are related in exactly the same way. Calculate the number to complete the third group and write it in the brackets.

Example: (3 [6] 9)   (8 [9] 10)   (6 [**8**] 10)

94.   (25 [40] 15)   (64 [80] 16)   (30 [   ] 10)

95.   (9 [26] 15)   (14 [27] 11)   (19 [   ] 19)

96.   (8 [48] 6)   (9 [54] 6)   (7 [   ] 6)

97.   (62 [51] 8)   (27 [18] 6)   (43 [   ] 14)

98.   (8 [26] 9)   (7 [23] 8)   (14 [   ] 4)

99.   (32 [2] 8)   (22 [1] 11)   (64 [   ] 8)

100.   (4 [32] 4)   (7 [84] 6)   (11 [   ] 3)

94.	....
95.	....
96.	....
97.	....
98.	....
99.	....
100.	....

✓	This page
Total	14

THIS IS THE LAST PAGE

ANSWERS

AND

PROGRESS RECORD SHEET

Answers to Practice Paper 1

#	Answer	#	Answer	#	Answer
1.	hear	35.	10	68.	K
2.	sand	36.	0	69.	15
3.	eyes	37.	0	70.	0
4.	seat	38.	100	71.	48
5.	neat	39.	8762	72.	10
6.	here	40.	FADE	73.	3
7.	snow	41.	2453	74.	5
8.	FIGHT & RICE	42.	LEAF	75.	10
9.	HEAR & THEM	43.	5493	76.	ULFH
10.	EACH & TABLE	44.	LANE	77.	FRUIT
11.	MOTH & PROUD	45.	D	78.	LSPQCQ
12.	ARROW & BRAIN	46.	Carlos	79.	QSYWI
13.	HEIR & STEAM	47.	war	80.	PLAYER
14.	RIGHT & BOLD	48.	rip	81.	NQWLJX
15.	scrape & graze	49.	rid	82.	MOLE
16.	cease & stop	50.	ten	83.	QHCEU
17.	descend & fall	51.	ear	84.	BADGE
18.	gleam & glisten	52.	ill	85.	27
19.	describe & explain	53.	din	86.	11
20.	broad & wide	54.	MR	87.	16
21.	reply & answer	55.	FW	88.	17
22.	competitor & contestant	56.	KR	89.	10
23.	fare-well	57.	QF	90.	240
24.	clam-our	58.	MN	91.	46
25.	deter-mined	59.	JZ	92.	19
26.	beg-in	60.	VW	93.	LAST
27.	cart-ridge	61.	B	94.	MEAL
28.	shop-ping	62.	T	95.	NEAT
29.	tar-get	63.	T	96.	SALE
30.	for-tune	64.	F	97.	RUST
31.	4	65.	L	98.	TONE
32.	96	66.	W	99.	MEAL
33.	200	67.	T	100.	MICE
34.	14				

Answers to Practice Paper 2

1.	27	35.	land	68.	XM
2.	12	36.	vest	69.	IP
3.	48	37.	star	70.	QG
4.	29	38.	C	71.	knows & male
5.	26	39.	12.30 pm	72.	kettle & jug
6.	72	40.	8	73.	station & dock
7.	4	41.	60	74.	pair & trio
8.	17	42.	20	75.	hare & fox
9.	LY	43.	16	76.	left & down
10.	KZ	44.	6	77.	set & nest
11.	TQ	45.	400	78.	12
12.	VJ	46.	0	79.	9
13.	XN	47.	20	80.	50
14.	JD	48.	art	81.	8
15.	UQ	49.	rip	82.	1
16.	onion & broccoli	50.	tip	83.	52
17.	cows & sheep	51.	inn	84.	71
18.	crab & heron	52.	ten	85.	scar-let
19.	horse & pig	53.	ear	86.	part-ridge
20.	rock & boat	54.	led	87.	pop-pies
21.	architect & joiner	55.	PEAL	88.	car-pet
22.	kilo & yard	56.	LEAN	89.	can-on
23.	oppose & support	57.	STAB	90.	off-ice
24.	superior & inferior	58.	BOAT	91.	slit-her
25.	comic & serious	59.	PEEP	92.	spar-row
26.	despair & hope	60.	DARE	93.	QNXY
27.	level & uneven	61.	SEAT	94.	HOUSE
28.	supple & rigid	62.	ROOK	95.	URCEG
29.	opaque & clear	63.	CE	96.	TNLQJ
30.	tidiness & disorder	64.	QK	97.	GERBIL
31.	west	65.	AO	98.	RHRHOS
32.	peal	66.	PJ	99.	HBUWI
33.	even	67.	MD	100.	PASTA
34.	heat				

Answers to Practice Paper 3

1.	East & right	35.	his	68.	CM
2.	way & site	36.	one	69.	VJ
3.	shortest & youngest	37.	low	70.	SC
4.	France & Belgium	38.	EAST & DENY	71.	TB
5.	bird & bee	39.	LIMB & CRATE	72.	RL
6.	read & measure	40.	CAVE & RICE	73.	GX
7.	bull & gander	41.	BLOW & KNOWN	74.	HC
8.	post	42.	RIDE & GEAR	75.	RU
9.	ground	43.	HERO & CROWN	76.	NKPM
10.	dart	44.	GRIN & ROAD	77.	DRIVE
11.	stalk	45.	2	78.	BREAD
12.	bolt	46.	16	79.	HORSES
13.	coast	47.	8	80.	COTJUC
14.	graze	48.	72	81.	DPCXFC
15.	stable	49.	10	82.	COUNT
16.	hear	50.	240	83.	QQJMU
17.	seal	51.	1	84.	STRING
18.	went	52.	32	85.	LIST
19.	dear	53.	6793	86.	WIND
20.	tall	54.	TREAT	87.	OPEN
21.	nose	55.	2379	88.	LIFT
22.	term	56.	TART	89.	SLIP
23.	dormant & asleep	57.	1972	90.	RISK
24.	sturdy & solid	58.	FARMER	91.	COAT
25.	drag & haul	59.	4371	92.	LOST
26.	reduce & decrease	60.	Danielle & Steven	93.	29
27.	bend & stoop	61.	3.45 pm	94.	9
28.	join & connect	62.	robin & sparrow	95.	12
29.	tidy & neat	63.	bird & squirrel	96.	12
30.	shout & exclaim	64.	paper & book	97.	12
31.	ten	65.	flower & sycamore	98.	22
32.	low	66.	London & Manchester	99.	36
33.	war	67.	ewe & cow	100.	11
34.	cod				

Answers to Practice Paper 4

1.	10	35.	13	68.	BROOK
2.	66	36.	30	69.	QVFDZ
3.	24	37.	2	70.	Annabelle
4.	13	38.	14	71.	LEAD & PRAISE
5.	42	39.	9	72.	PLAN & TALE
6.	1	40.	LJ	73.	HAIR & CLOCK
7.	43	41.	VH	74.	CARE & STARVE
8.	FOLD	42.	LD	75.	RING & BROOM
9.	MARE	43.	BG	76.	EASE & DRAFT
10.	NOSE	44.	DP	77.	ALLOW & FEEL
11.	PART	45.	LU	78.	far-thing
12.	SAFE	46.	KS	79.	cash-mere
13.	MEAN	47.	teacher & pupil	80.	high-way
14.	DALE	48.	Germany & European	81.	wool-lens
15.	CAKE	49.	leaf & flower	82.	in-vest
16.	15	50.	glider & aeroplane	83.	out-rage
17.	40	51.	lion & mouse	84.	gear-box
18.	120	52.	measure & acre	85.	back-ward
19.	20	53.	circle & oval	86.	DZ
20.	40	54.	shrewd & stupid	87.	IS
21.	1	55.	glum & cheerful	88.	BO
22.	20	56.	combine & disperse	89.	KK
23.	6	57.	courageous & cowardly	90.	FN
24.	3	58.	create & destroy	91.	CD
25.	25	59.	glossy & dull	92.	OF
26.	15	60.	allow & prohibit	93.	BR
27.	32	61.	true & inaccurate	94.	track & road
28.	3	62.	AFPE	95.	knows & right
29.	5	63.	GOLD	96.	football & tennis
30.	5	64.	UJBDP	97.	three & two
31.	14	65.	CANDY	98.	bee & cow
32.	B	66.	HAPPY	99.	slow & tiny
33.	6	67.	RPGKO	100.	waited & hurried
34.	9				

Answers to Practice Paper 5

1.	NS	35.	maximum & slowest	68.	pull-over
2.	QR	36.	nail & wood	69.	he-art
3.	QK	37.	lion & fish	70.	over-look
4.	ZA	38.	wrong & lose	71.	ancient & old
5.	EP	39.	found & laughed	72.	often & frequent
6.	DT	40.	WD	73.	confident & optimistic
7.	OJ	41.	HG	74.	replica & copy
8.	Jenny	42.	DX	75.	sombre & dismal
9.	D	43.	CD	76.	fault & defect
10.	car	44.	FL	77.	wise & astute
11.	rid	45.	VI	78.	sound & secure
12.	one	46.	VC	79.	18
13.	hat	47.	OC	80.	9
14.	toe	48.	lion & monkey	81.	21
15.	rot	49.	train & aeroplane	82.	1
16.	den	50.	Paris & London	83.	2
17.	ham	51.	nut & bolt	84.	8
18.	test	52.	leaf & root	85.	2
19.	term	53.	cereal & potatoes	86.	4
20.	rent	54.	sailor & captain	87.	23
21.	fort	55.	B	88.	7
22.	nest	56.	L	89.	64
23.	land	57.	H	90.	16
24.	sold	58.	M	91.	23
25.	EACH & BREAD	59.	R	92.	3
26.	ABLE & TRIP	60.	Y	93.	27
27.	WATER & MAID	61.	P	94.	40
28.	PLAN & EVENT	62.	K	95.	40
29.	ARROW & MALE	63.	coo-king	96.	42
30.	FAME & FRIGHT	64.	tea-ring	97.	26
31.	LOWER & RAFT	65.	break-fast	98.	22
32.	bus & rocket	66.	arc-her	99.	4
33.	cricket & golf	67.	with-out	100.	66
34.	school & hospital				

Progress Record Sheet

Practice Paper 1

Date completed: ....

Page	1	2	3	4	5	6	7	8	TOTAL
Possible	14	16	8	8	14	15	9	16	100
Score									

Practice Paper 2

Date completed: ....

Page	1	2	3	4	5	6	7	8	TOTAL
Possible	15	15	9	8	15	15	15	8	100
Score									

Practice Paper 3

Date completed: ....

Page	1	2	3	4	5	6	7	8	TOTAL
Possible	15	15	14	8	9	14	9	16	100
Score									

Practice Paper 4

Date completed: ....

Page	1	2	3	4	5	6	7	8	TOTAL
Possible	15	8	9	14	15	9	15	15	100
Score									

Practice Paper 5

Date completed: ....

Page	1	2	3	4	5	6	7	TOTAL
Possible	9	15	15	15	16	16	14	100
Score								